How to Analyze People

Dark Psychology

*Secret Techniques to Analyze and
Influence Anyone Using Body Language,
Human Psychology and Personality Types*

The follow Book is reproduced below with the goal of providing information that is as accurate and reliable as possible. Regardless, purchasing this Book can be seen as consent to the fact that both the publisher and the author of this book are in no way experts on the topics discussed within and that any recommendations or suggestions that are made herein are for entertainment purposes only. Professionals should be consulted as needed prior to undertaking any of the action endorsed herein.

This declaration is deemed fair and valid by both the American Bar Association and the Committee of Publishers Association and is legally binding throughout the United States.

Furthermore, the transmission, duplication or reproduction of any of the following work including specific information will be considered an illegal act irrespective of if it is done electronically or in print. This extends to creating a secondary or tertiary copy of the work or a recorded copy and is only allowed with express written consent from the Publisher. All additional right reserved.

The information in the following pages is broadly considered to be a truthful and accurate account of facts and as such any inattention, use or misuse of the information in question by the reader will render any resulting actions solely under their

Table of Contents

Introduction 1

Chapter 1: Analyzing People Using Body Language 4

Chapter 2: Manipulation 29

Chapter 3: NLP 42

Chapter 4: Deception 57

Conclusion 70

Thank you 73

Introduction

Congratulations on purchasing *How to Analyze People: Dark Psychology - Secret Techniques to Analyze and Influence Anyone Using Body Language, Human Psychology, and Personality Types* and thank you for doing so.

The following chapters will discuss how to analyze a person and make them do what you want them to do, nothing more and nothing less. In today's society, having an edge on social interactions can benefit you in many ways. Whether you are networking, pitching an idea, or simply trying to get your way, this book will help you learn techniques, teach you how to influence different types of people, and understand what makes them tick. You will learn how to take what you observe about others and influence them to do what you want. Along the way, you will learn more about yourself, as you learn about others. A word to the wise, what follows in this book, if used in the wrong way could get you in a lot of trouble.

I have compiled techniques that I have learned in my life by studying an endless list of influential people, watching how politicians wave their agenda around in a form of hypnosis by paying special attention to advertisements, among a million other creative ways for me to become a master of my universe. I have been using the techniques for many years and believed in them. I analyze every situation for an opportunity to apply these skills, and it has paid off in my life. I write with the purpose for you to help yourself and get what you want, but the techniques can be used for the sole benefit of your subject as you wish.

There are plenty of books on this subject on the market and thank you again for choosing this one.

Every effort was made to ensure it is full of as much useful information as possible, please enjoy.

Chapter 1
Analyzing People Using Body Language

The same way you train a dog to listen to your body language and cues, you can train a human being to follow you without question. Now there are some people out there who would automatically say that blind obedience is a dangerous thing, this book is not for them. Rather, this book is for those who understand the potential benefits associated with a little absolute control and are willing to do what is required to make that dream a reality.

This won't happen automatically, of course, few things worth having are obtained easily after all, but with practice, you will be able to subtly exert your will on those around you for your own ends. The first step to control those around you lies in analyzing them, however, which is why this chapter will discuss how to analyze people based on their body language.

Four temperaments

Generally speaking, there are four main personality types, and understanding which classification your current target falls under is crucial to approaching them effectively. Historically speaking, these personality types include sanguine (enthusiastic, active, and social), choleric (short-tempered, fast, or irritable), melancholic (analytical, wise, and quiet), and phlegmatic (relaxed and peaceful).

Dr. Helen Fisher has updated this traditional theory to develop modern names for the same fundamental personality types. She says the four personality types are: The Explorer (Sanguine); The Negotiator (Phlegmatic); The Director

(Choleric); and the Builder (Melancholic). Now, this is not to say that those you encounter may not have a mix of these personality types, but nevertheless, they are sure to have a dominant type that you can play off of.

While at first knowing the various types of personalities won't do you much good, with practice you will find that you can attach common personality quirks to each of them. Eventually, you will be able to walk into a room of people you don't know and pick out the basic personality of each person just by observing them.

While initially, you might feel nervous, if you instead make a point of focusing on the body language of those around you and try to pinpoint what type of personality you are dealing with. You might notice the people around you are not exactly at ease, or perhaps some of the people around you seem to be beaming with confidence. You will watch and listen. It is time to train the dog.

Choleric: Generally speaking, you should be able to pick out any cholerics in the room as they are the ones who cannot sit still. If you hope to successfully influence this person, then you are going to need to be prepared to make up for their lack of patience. You can usually hear the choleric person before you see them which is a sign they are in a good mood. It does not take much to get this person's attention because they are happy to give it.

You may find that you have the most difficulty with this personality type as they tend to want to share their passions with others which means they are often naturally charismatic. They may even naturally dominate other personality types, especially phlegmatic individuals which means you are going to need to deal with them first if you are in a group setting. They tend to be natural planners which means they will go along with what you say if you present it as a logical solution to a specific problem.

The biggest weakness of many choleric individuals is that they can become depressed or moody when their plans don't come together. Thus, a natural way to get them off their guard is to either mention how they are about to fail or to bring up a particularly painful failure from the past. Additionally, you will want to keep in mind that they are often impatient, anxious and generally have a hard time relaxing. If you come across a choleric individual, you can ingratiate yourself by playing to these weaknesses or you can exploit them if you have something else in mind.

Another dead giveaway that you are dealing with a choleric person is that they tend to be less emotional than the other personality types. This means they are more likely to be unsympathetic if you play to their emotions and are more likely to be inflexible in general. As such, you will need to appeal to their logic if you hope to make progress. You can use this lack of emotion to your advantage as well, however, as cholerics are often uncomfortable around excessive displays of emotion.

Phlegmatic: On the other side of the scale are the phlegmatic individuals as they are going to be the ones that seem to be the most content with whatever is currently taking place. They will likely be at ease with you or anyone else who approaches them, and you will need to match their wavelength in order to make positive headway with them. One of the best things about phlegmatics is that they are consistent which means that once you convince them to come around to your way of thinking, you won't have to worry about doing it again. They are also naturally affable and prefer to reconcile differences if possible. They are often shy, however, which means they may freeze up if you come at them directly.

Phlegmatic individuals tend to prefer stability to change which means they are often susceptible to ideas that involve remaining with the status quo.

As such, if you are ever going to convince them to go against the grain you are going to need to move slowly and get them to understand that they really have no other options. Keep in mind that they can be passive aggressive and don't respond in kind, this is only a response to their dislike of change and is more of an automatic response than anything else.

These types of people often keep their emotions hidden and put forth a relaxed and easy-going façade, regardless of what is going on inside. As such, it is going to take some extra effort to crack their shell and learn how they are really feeling. You may want to engage them in broad conversation to see if you can get a sense of what makes them happy and what makes them angry. Moving forward without this bellwether can be dangerous as it will be difficult to know if they like what you are saying or are opposed to it. While they are often willing to compromise rather than make a scene, they are often quite selfish and will resent any concessions they have to make. Don't forget they have no problem holding grudges.

Melancholic: The melancholic people in the room are likely going to be the ones looking back at you as you look at them. They are the ones who are most likely to be wary of you right off the bat so before you deal with them it is important to plan for resistance. These individuals are often given to deep thought, while still being sensitive to the thoughts and wills of others. This can cause them to focus too much on the innate cruelty in the world which can easily lead to bouts of depression.

One useful trait that most melancholics share is a desire for perfection in all they do which makes them highly conscientious of others. This is directly at odds with the difficulty they often have relating to other people, as they often fail to live up to the melancholic's standards. They are typically very independent and prefer to do things for themselves rather than settling for less than they believe they deserve.

As such, the best way to ingratiate yourself to a melancholic is to appeal to the sense of self-worth that comes along to their perfectionism. If you can find something that allows you access to their ivory tower, then they will naturally be far more inclined to follow your lead; after all, you've proven you have taste. They also only tend to focus on one thing at a time, which means you may need to lead the conversation in order to ensure that it gets to where you need it to be.

Sanguine: Sanguine individuals are known to be charismatic, impulsive and, above all, pleasure-seeking. If you are at a social gathering, then the sanguine individuals will be the loudest ones in the room making friends with everyone else. These personality types often have difficulty following through on tasks, however, which means that a great way to ingratiate yourself to them is by helping them complete the things they totally mean to finish but have not yet gotten around to.

It is very difficult to embarrass a sanguine individual, as they are typically shameless by nature and are always certain that whatever they are doing is the right choice. They are also virtually endless wells of confidence which means you will never make any headway with them by trying to convince them that they have made a wrong move.

They tend to be very physical and enjoy personal contact which means that matching this desire is a great way to score bonus points right out of the gate. They are also naturally curious which means you can also hook them early by showing them something they have never seen before, or at least promising to. They also love to tell stories which means listening and commenting when appropriate is another great ingratiation technique.

The biggest weakness of sanguine individuals is that they tend to feel controlled by their circumstances. As such, if you can convince them that the best way out of the latest situation they have found themselves in then they will likely go along with whatever it is you are suggesting without a second thought. If you are in a social situation you will want to get them on your side early as they will be more than happy to spread the news of how great you are to everyone else at the party.

What to do with this detail: Knowing the different personality types will help you read people to decide who they really are. From here, you can decide what technique will be needed to persuade them or relax them for your own purposes.

Positive body language

Positive body language gives off a good vibe or energy that those you are speaking with will instinctively seek more of. Likewise, others will get a good feeling when you're around. A very telling sign of positive body language is if someone leans towards you when they speak or lean into a conversation. If this happens naturally, you are dealing with a "Phlegmatic" person. These are usually a very confident people; get to know your type. It is a small display of intimacy and can be taken advantage of regardless of their confidence. Give off a little laugh and a genuine smile to reciprocate the trust. It should not be hard after that to trust that person or to gain their trust.

Another sign of positive body language is when a person seems effortlessly relaxed without crossing their arms or legs. This screams, "I am confident," when the truth is, they likely have a low self-image, despite displaying total confidence. Despite appearances, these individuals tend to fall into the melancholic type of personality.

There is a chance that you or someone you are observing is feeling insecure and trying to mask it. However, if you are not dealing with the melancholic personality, you might be dealing with a choleric personality. Everyone has heard the phrase "Fake it until you make it." This is the dogma of the choleric personality type. Whether they were cut out for something or not, they will not give up easily.

If you are confronting this type of personality, simply the mere act of uncrossing your arms or legs should gain you a little confidence. Add to that a genuine smile for the next person that you encounter and watch as they lighten up a bit in response. It might take a little practice, but this type of body language gives you control of the situation.

Understanding eye contact: This one can be tricky as it is easy to misinterpret but long eye contact is almost always meaningful in some way shape or form. If a person can look at you without looking away for more than a few seconds, then usually they are confident around you and are likely to be genuine. This is likely to be your phlegmatic personality type; one who is displaying a little bit of awkward shyness. They will notice you scanning the room, but do not count on them calling you out on this.

Typically, eye contact can make you look interested and says a lot about the person you are dealing with. If you find yourself being stared at by a person, you are likely dealing with a sanguine personality. This personality type is an observer and tends to be the sincerest of the four. By looking people in the eye, it is their way of proving those qualities.

Depending on the situation, you can look down and away out of shyness. When people are shy, they are deemed innocent. Your phlegmatic personalities are really good at this as well. You want to seem innocent, no matter what your intentions as the best choice for drawing other people in is to keep them interested. Since you want people to trust you, you have to get close enough to analyze what type of personality you are dealing with.

If the other party looks away and down, and then back up at you, take advantage of this opportunity to consider them more closely. This is a sign of vulnerability which means they trust you, so you are free to do with that trust what you may. This is often a good time to ask them about themselves or offer something personal to break the ice. Compliments are always a good choice as it is hard to dislike someone who has recently payed you a compliment.

Smile: The most important asset anyone has is their smile. A smile is a window to the soul. If you are walking down the street and someone gives you a genuine smile, it can change your day. That is the power you want to carry around with you. This is the gift of most sanguine personality types. They are cheerful on the outside and can easily make people laugh. Faking a smile is hard. The truth of any smile lies in the eyes. Pay careful attention to the lines that form when the cheeks rise as the evidence of a genuine smile forms.

If you ask someone to do something and they decline, smile anyway, they will feel bad for saying no. Depending on their actual reaction, say it again in a different way and in a cartoonish voice (humor), and follow up with a serious voice. Ask for the favor again by adding another smile. This is best used in social situations and is to be avoided at work. Unless you are super cool with your co-workers or if you are sure you are dealing with a sanguine personality.

If your co-worker or your boss display a dislike for emotions or seem impatient, you could be dealing with a choleric personality. You will need to make it seem like they are the leaders. You're pushing boundaries, but you don't want anyone to recognize this game. No matter how it ends, do not give too much of a reaction. If you are too happy, it could kill the vibe. The same is true if you are too upset, just smile. You will not be able to change your own personality type as the theory is that you were born that way. However, knowing more about yourself, you can control the display, or even master your weaknesses to have influence or get close enough to other people, that you may sincerely analyze them.

Negative personality cues

Now that you have a basic understanding of positive body language, let us look at the opportunity to dig into the negative cues often given by different personality types. Sometimes even the most trustworthy and genuine people can give off signals of distress through body cues, so it is important to take them with a grain of salt to avoid being misled.

If you find someone who is trying to discourage you, or they are judging you, it is likely that their personality is phlegmatic If the negativity you are picking up on is coming from someone who is demanding attention or seems phony, you are amidst a sanguine personality type. You want to know the difference and how to respond to either situation to achieve a goal. Whether it is to cheer someone up, so you can enjoy their company or perhaps you need to get away from someone who would seek to destroy your aura. Either way, practice makes perfect, and observing takes a lot of it.

Personal space: If someone moves away from you, this is often a sign that they believe you either did something wrong or you represent something negative to them. This mentality applies to all four of the personality types. It hurts to feel rejected. Instead of feeling sorry for yourself, move back into their realm if you want to change the vibe.

Your sanguine personality types will not move away from you. They like to be close to the person they are listening to. Do not let this throw you off. Insist that you are worth it. Don't say it, but simply adjust your posture to a very relaxed position. You can do this by pointing your feet at that person, smiling and either asking a question about their job or what city they are from. From here, still smiling, ask if they want to get some fresh air. You have now created an intimate moment with someone who wasn't so sure about you. Let your sanguine personality do a lot of the talking if they do walk out the door with you as there is a good chance they will take a walk with you because they are restless.

Defuse a negative situation: If you need to stay cool until you can make an exit in a tough situation, avoid smiling. This occurs where someone is giving the impression that they are unstable or unsafe. Although, they are likely to be sanguine personality which is also known for turning people off, try to distinguish if they are angry or actually going to zap you of your will to live. What you need to do is avoid staring at the person but to make a few seconds of eye contact and act like everything is fine. This is an extreme example, but if someone had a gun to your head, you do not want to freak out and cry. Rather, you would want to stay calm, cool, and collected. This is the strength of a phlegmatic personality type.

Crying and carrying on, would irritate the person and they might lose their cool and shoot you. This could happen if they are a choleric personality type, which has an extreme distaste for tears and is unsympathetic towards other in general. in intense situations as it tends to make people a little calmer and more likely to bend to your will.

Looking side to side: Whether in a social setting or a professional setting, whoever you are dealing with should not be looking side to side. This means they are uncomfortable or bored. Are they coming across as guarded? A melancholic personality type may seem guarded when they are truly just in their own world. If you are confronted with this situation, use the opportunity to display positive body language to gain control of the vibe.

Don't force the person to look at you by demanding attention. The melancholic personality usually has a complex and will see you as a threat. Therefore, keep your arms uncrossed and smile when you get a glance. At some point, it is good to ask a question. This gives the person a chance to forget that they are uncomfortable. This person just needs to know that they are not alone and that you have something to offer.

Touching their face: If a person is rubbing their face, they are not comfortable. This is a trait of the choleric personality type. They cannot sit still, and maybe they have extreme anxiety. This is prevalent in today's society, but the real culprit may just be that they are impatient. The best thing you can do to gain control to get this person to respond to you is to act tired. Lethargy is not an emotional state of mind, which is important for this personality type who is very unemotional.

While it may sound crazy, if you are tired, they think you do not notice that they are antsy or sweaty, or even that you are no threat. Pretending to be tired is a great defense to anything that you messed up. It might not appease your boss, but for most social situations, being tired is an out, because everyone can relate. Keep this tool, along with all the others in your mental toolbox.

Stress: Choleric personality types burn out easily from trying to always maintain control. Stressed people are easily conned, flattered, or manipulated. If you really need something from someone, wait for a moment when they are stressed out. At this moment, they will not want to argue. They may not have the energy to think things through, and you have the prime opportunity. The key to this is remaining calm and to not let them abuse you. Since you do not want to be blamed for the stress, you just want to be served by it. Keep in mind, that this personality type almost always needs to blame someone else for their problems.

Not only can you persuade a person easier when they are stressed you can also become a hero. You know that this person needs reassurance, especially your melancholic personality type. They need more reassurance than any other personality type, as they are clothed in self-doubt. They need protection from any more stress, and you offer to provide a relaxing environment. This is where flattery comes in. Lay it on. Now drenched in your sugary sweet attitude, ask for what you want. Let your voice be a little hesitant. This person will fear you leaving them. Just keep a person chasing their own tale for long enough to achieve your goal.

Have a goal in mind

With all the advice being given, choose your intention before applying any techniques. Before you can persuade someone to act differently, you will need to dig into their world and find out why they are resisting you. Once you know their fear or motivation, you can minimize the risk. Does your intention involve exploring? You can target a sanguine personality, known for having the curiosity of a child.

Are you planning on negotiating a deal? This will be easiest with a phlegmatic personality type who is pretty agreeable hiding the fact that they have no goals of their own. Do you need someone to take responsibility for something you need to be done? Surely, you can easily convince the compulsive and "bossy" choleric personality type that this was their idea. Do you need a loyal person to achieve your goal? Find a melancholic personality. This is the reason they get up in the morning, to prove that they are trustworthy and self-sacrificing.

No matter what personality type you are dealing with, you are better off if they can't explain the reason for not agreeing with you or rejecting your influence. Shake your head and act a little disappointed. If they get an attitude or want to argue, always, and I mean always, take the high road and clean up the mess by using phrases like, "I respect your opinion or belief, our friendship is not worth losing. I apologize. I am going to reconsider your position. Really, I am." Use a genuine tone. Whether or not you mean what you are saying, you are gaining the reputation as someone who is serious, and for that, you will have respect.

Chapter 2

Manipulation

Once you have gotten a decent read on a person, the next step to mastering your environment and analyzing your potential in each situation is learning how to manipulate another person's feelings and reactions through more subtle cues, both verbal and non-verbal. This will create an environment where your suggestions can thrive.

Don't beat yourself up for thinking outside the box when it comes to analyzing and influencing people. While some people might call it manipulation, you can simply tell them that you are extremely persuasive. What's more, there is nothing to say that the person you are influencing wasn't waiting for an excuse to move forward in the direction you suggested anyway. It is your creativity in constructing a good plan or formula that turns resistance into compliance.

Manipulation Basics

The art of manipulation lies in the engrained principals of protecting and nourishing other people, both of which forms a quick emotional bond. It is important to keep in mind that the stronger the emotion you can make another person feel, the easier it will be to bend them to your will. Emotion is what controls the world, gain control over your own, practice reading people, and learn how to persuade and analyze and you will be well on your way to manipulating others successfully.

Besides emotion, successful manipulation is all about the imbalance of power. There may be times when getting what you want from another person means using the home court advantage which means keeping the person in an environment in which you have primary control. This includes your home, car, office, or even your side of town. This makes it harder for your target to do things such as dodge a conversation or even make a decision that they think might hurt your feelings.

While it may seem surprising, letting another person dominate the conversation is a good thing when you want to have the upper hand with them. You can establish their underlying weaknesses and their strengths by listening to their stories and throwing in a few questions from time to time, which will also ingratiate you to them further as it makes you seem as though you are supremely interested in what they have to say. You aren't going to want to let the conversation feel one sided, however, which means you will want to tell them enough about your situation to make them feel comfortable while at the same time withholding any information that would weaken your standpoint or that could be contorted to mean something else. Don't be afraid to lie to protect any weaknesses in your argument.

If someone is pushing you for more than they need, you can use a humble tone, and explain that there are things about you no one would understand, or that you aren't interesting enough to warrant talking about. This will make them curious, and it will also make them a little nurturing, which is where you can snag them. This is known as flipping the script and it can be a very effective technique when used selectively.

If you have to, speak about facts and statistics. Ramble about as many as you can to be a bit overwhelming. At this time, you need to show interest on their part but establish that if you are to go along with whatever they are suggesting, then you are going to have your own rules. Depending on the situation you are currently in, this may be enough for them to "decide" to complete the task in question for you or to give in to your suggestion because it is easier than going along with your stipulations.

Another way to manipulate a person is to change the modulation of your voice. If you are trying to intimidate a person, you will want to be loud. If you are seeking sympathy, lose the loud tone for a depressed, defeated tone instead. Most people are inclined to help a person who is feeling down. Now that you have their sympathy, ask for something. Suggest what you want in a way that seems impossible to achieve. Wait for their response, which should be some variation of, "I want to help you." Some people will want to offer up advice as a way to soothe you. To avoid losing control of the situation you will need to consider their advice and find a reason that their logic is faulty to ensure things remain under your control.

Manipulation tools for specific situations
A key to pulling off any form of manipulation is to see what drives the person you are dealing with.

For example, is it a religion? If so, you would need to focus on their devotion and find a creative way to get your point across using their religion. It is a good way to reinforce their opinion of themselves which is most likely that they are godly and intelligent. As long as you focus on their utopian visions and aspirations, you will find this technique to be very effective.

Another tool that is useful from time to time is sarcasm. It allows you to express your discontent with someone while maintaining a doorway out as if you were just joking. But be cautious, as sarcasm can be insulting and hurtful if misused. After you have been given the chance to vent, turn it around to the sarcastic "what if." This allows the person to hear your opinion, and it comes across like you are just defeated. Now they can save you. When they offer their help, humbly tell them it is not their responsibility, but that you do need their support. It is helpful to add, "What would I do without you?"

You must keep in mind that you are being manipulated every day. The news, media, and those in power all deploy tactics to keep your attention or threaten your security for non-compliance. You are bombarded with images and stories that tug at your heart, anger your soul, and move you either into action or into seclusion. Just seeing how easily you can have the same effect on a person, will allow you to recognize when it is being done to you. Awareness is life changing. It is at this moment that you realize you have tried conventional methods of persuasion, being genuine and truly caring. Previously, you got nothing in return, but you will from now on.

Be creative

You will need to focus on your creativity for these manipulative tactics. Your goal is to transform someone's reality and alter their beliefs. Every situation is different which means you will need to be creative and think on your feet. You must observe the cues a person is giving you. You must observe their reactions to you and to others, as these can be very telling. Sometimes, just watching your target interact with others can give you more insight on how to manipulate them.

For example, if you see how a coworker reacted to a customer, you can use that to make them feel justified by adding your opinion as an out to explain how they reacted. They will repeat the excuse you provided them. This can be used against them later. If you are trying to get them to do something for you, just point out how they overreacted to that customer which should shame them into following your suggestion. They should act in the way you suggest to minimize their past actions.

Sometimes all you have to do is create an image. Think of a spin on something that would suggest the person you are dealing with is a victim. Encourage them to see how others have been unappreciative and lazy compared to them. Suggest a course of action and reap the benefits.

If you are dying to know what someone feels about a situation, for example in politics or religion, make up a story that you read on the internet that is sure to rile them up. Sit back and watch their reaction and start agreeing with them. Be sure to add your perspective to draw them out of the shocking story into your plan. You might just be harvesting information to keep a profile on someone who is a threat to your vision of success. Building your profile, you will be able to understand their weakness in most situations.

Take your time

You can be sure to pay special attention to their strengths and find ways to undermine them. Don't take it so far as to where others observing can figure out what your intentions are, and instead always take the high road in public so that at the end of the day, most people will only ever see the public face you decide to show them.

Keep in mind that everyone really just wants to be happy which means they seek to have understanding and supportive people around them. They think it is rare for someone to take an interest in them without wanting something in return. This is where patience becomes your ally. You cannot really act like someone has to be available at a moment's notice. Anyone can figure out that you have selfish motives if you display this impatient tendency. It might be killing you to lie in wait for the perfect opportunity, but it would kill you more to be seen as a fake. So, wait. Even encourage them to ask others about the situation. Once you have proven that you are only worried about them or want to see them succeed, then you can wiggle into their mind with subtle manipulation.

While playing on the heartstrings of another, you weaken their response. You cannot simply ignore that they might say no to your request or idea. You have to come across as sincere in trying to help or care about them. Find a way to make their "no" seem unreasonable without saying it directly. You will have to point out that if someone else acted like they did, with their closed mind, they would see it as being stubborn or pig-headed. Let them know that the brain has a chemical response to doing something new and brave. Tell them that the brain lights up like a Christmas tree when changes are occurring.

The bottom line is that there is potential in manipulation. It is a creative process. It takes a little planning and observing. But if mastered, it can change your life. You will feel powerful every day. You will start to see every rejection as a canvas. It is your starting point. A word for word or gesture by gesture guarantee that you are in control.

Self- preservation is an important aspect of manipulation. You do not want to be seen as a manipulator. You want to be known as the neutral person who sees all sides but uses logic to decide why your decision is more valid. Maintain a solid reputation for being thoughtful and people will seek your opinion often. This is an advantage from the start. In a new group of people, you can find a way to agree with everyone, and make a statement that you were always taught to show respect and think of all sides before making a decision. This could have the others taking your point into consideration just because you were willing to do this for them. This becomes your thoughtful reputation.

There are many forms of manipulation which actually can benefit you and your target. You cannot feel guilty for taking drastic measures to appeal to their dark psychosis. It is for everyone and can hardly be avoided. It is time for you to recognize the signs of it happening to you and take control of the situation. Start to think that when a person says no, they are being self-destructive. They will need you to help them think for themselves. In the end, they might even thank you for your help, as if they were just struggling until you came along with a solution. After you accomplish your goal, make a statement about how much calmer and happier they seem now that they have tried new things as it reinforces your behavior.

Chapter 3

NLP

NLP stands for Neuro-Linguistic Programming. NLP can more easily be explained as a roadmap for the brain. Supporters of NLP believe that the way people act and feel is based on their perception of the world around them. Your subconscious mind is the part of the brain with the main goal of getting you what it perceives you want. You may even be barely aware of what is taking place, you are just programmed by what you have already concluded about the world.

But hold on! You can change this aspect of yourself, and you can change it in other people too. The subconscious mind is only trying to serve you what your conscious mind thinks about and wants.

The fact of the matter is that the world most people inhabit is quite a bit different from the world that actually exists. What version have you been led to believe? What version will you force on others?

To understand what the subconscious wants, you have to know what it has been fed. Everyone will have their own world inside them. It will depend on how the five senses are stimulated. Your nervous system will delete anything that your mind cannot handle. What is left is the reduction of the world into smaller segments that are easier to deal with. You can identify what a person has reduced their world to be by seeing what they pay attention to most readily.

If you can alter a person's perception, you can ultimately alter their view of the world. This is a life-changing realization because you can get them to act out in such a way that their subconscious mind will go to work. This occurs by believing that this is what the person wants based on their experience. You can control a person's emotional state using this fact.

The chains that you secure or break free from are at your command by paying attention to what language you have wrapped around them. Use words that generalize, delete someone's perception, or distort their perception based on what you learned by observing them.

There should be no guilt associated with this technique, as it is used on you every day by salespeople, commercials, and politicians. They orchestrate an emotional reaction and attach their product, making you believe it is what you need. It is actually pretty disgusting how much effort goes into making us, good consumers. But, let's make the best of it and "flip the script" by using their techniques for our own personal gain.

Think, for a second, about the last time you bought something you did not need. There was some kind of emotional connection happening, and you ended up with the useless or unnecessary product. You most likely do not even remember why you bought it. That is the effect you will be able to have on others all you need to do is distort your target's sense of need, provide a new need-based off of their model of the world.

NLP offers a lot of advantages for getting what you want. Emotions are extremely fragile and impressionable. Each technique has its own purpose and should be thought about ahead of time before deployment as the stages discussed in this chapter are somewhat interchangeable. They can be moved around or implemented depending on what reaction you are receiving or depending on what goal you have in mind for your subject. Do not underestimate your subject. They might seem hesitant, but do not give up, this stuff works for everyone. You are going to make a representation of the world communicated with a rich and complex expression of your model world.

Getting started

At the beginning stage, you will want to start to slowly mimic your subject. You will do this for their mannerisms and even the type of speech they are using to ensure that the words you are conveying are essentially hearing an argument in their own words. Mimicking in this way will allow your argument to slip past their natural mental defenses because they will interpret it as a friendly thought. For example, if you are talking with someone who has an accent, without being too obvious or rude, add the sound patterns they use in your speech. You are essentially faking recognize social cues to cause your subject to open up and be more comfortable around you. You can use intuition and structure to make your goal and your subject connected to the message being communicated.

If you find yourself dealing with a visual person, they are focused on what they see or have seen. You will want to implement your stories and use them as visual metaphors. Some of the phrases you might want to use are, "do you see what I mean?" or "look at it another way." This is engaging the core of how they communicate. Typically, when people feel like they do not have enough choices, paint the picture of a thousand choices, based on the model of the world you have chosen to deliver.

You might find out that the subject focuses on what they can hear. Auditory sensory motivation should be called upon if this is the case. Again, by paying attention to their own voice patterns, you can use phrases that speak to what they hear. For example, "I hear every word you say" or "before you judge, hear me out." When using this technique, pay attention to their eyes and reactions. Make a note of what direction they tend to look when listening to you. You will enrich your target's world by convincing them that they have a richer set of choices. Connect the value of the choices with their model of the world.

All you are trying to achieve at this moment is a solid link between the two of you. This will cause them to feel empathetic towards you, which will also cause them to lower their guard. A person usually comes to the conclusion that you are a good person because you have tapped into their psychological and emotional state. This is a stage of vulnerability. They are ripe for suggestion, but only if you can make it seem as though it is a part of their world view.

Making the next move

Once you have imitated their behavior, subtly change the language pattern that you use as a means to lead them to where you want them to be in that moment. Keep in mind, however, this is against their consent, which means that you MUST come across genuine using some of the techniques described in earlier chapters in order to break past their natural barriers. This is most helpful when it comes to trying to get someone to make a decision or finish something they have already started. Connect with the experience they are having right now by becoming them with your language or behavior.

Now it's time for conditioning. You will want to bait and hang your subject, metaphorically speaking of course. To bait, you will have used leading with physical gestures and speech to orchestrate an emotional state. For example, if you wanted to pass on an aggressive, stressed out emotional state you could speak quickly, touch your face more and use exaggerated hand gestures, while also indicating to them that time is of the essence. Once you have them baited, you will want to hang them with a physical cue, such as initiating physical contact. With practice, you can condition them to associate the mental state in question with the type of physical contact you have chosen. You can make them hungry. You could make them angry. You could make them laugh until they cry. The choice is yours.

You will need to continue to mimic their body language in order to drive this message home. You will want to copy their hand movements, the position of their feet, and look at everything they seem to look at, and so forth. Be careful again, if they are doing something really weird with their hands or feet, do not do the exact same thing as you will be caught. It is the same strategy with their gaze. If they are looking up and down, you could be noticed mimicking this, so just catch up when it seems they are a little more within normal range. They might have noticed it a bit, so just back off and start from scratch, ignoring every other gesture. Once you have had a chance to get them to let their guard down again, you can proceed in mimicking almost everything they do.

Wait until your subject is laughing really hard or getting really angry. This is a prime time to add your physical touch, to the shoulder, a pat on the back, or whatever you deem appropriate. You have just hung them again. Anytime you want to get them back into the emotional state of laughter or anger. This actually could be any heightened emotional state, but all you have to do is the touching, and like magic, they return to the state of mind you orchestrated.

A fascinating tip I want to share is how to be vague with the speech you are using. The vaguer you are, the odds that you will be able to successfully put them in a trance. Your words could literally mean anything. Take the word "strong" for example. It could apply to emotions, body, or a piece of wood. It is not the most descriptive word. Conversely, to remove the trance, use more specific words with a deeper meaning. For example, the word "silky," you know what it means no matter what you are describing. You know it will be soft and smooth.

That brings me to yet another one of my favorite tools in NLP, which is to be tolerant and carefree with the speech to influence your subject. It is easy to do but will still require practice. To implement this technique, you will want to have a handful of phrases that are suggestive, geared towards your goal. Here are a few of my favorite examples, "feel free to make yourself at home." Or "you are welcome to test it out first if you would like." This is securing a person's trust and permission to control how they feel.

Pay attention to your subject's eyes, as I mentioned earlier, try to gather a pattern of how they receive the information you are giving them. If they are against the information, what direction are their eyes moving? Look for the same pattern if they are enjoying the information. This is where you want to decide how to give them the information moving forward. Figure out what state of mind they would like to be in, based on their personality type and add to it accordingly. You will head in that direction first, secure your place in a relaxed and happy mode, and they will want to follow you there.

Do you want to give them the information in large quantity or do they react better to smaller chunks of information? Decide and dish it out accordingly. If you can dish out your information in smaller portions, it is more likely to be remembered. Sometimes a person might need more information to make a decision to be ready to give more if needed. Check to see if they generalize the topic. Generalizing prevents a person from making distinctions. This restricts their ability to see a wider range of choices, narrowing it down to those you have a direct influence on. Keep referencing whatever information they have provided you with and provide positive outcomes for the choices you provided. Wrap it in a story that you told, asking them to think of a time that they felt that way.

Final thoughts

The last few things I would like to mention on this subject is how to plot people against one another. This is another NLP programming pot of gold. Think about these scenarios: Mom v. Child; Husband v. Wife; Boss v. Employer, etc. Now think of stressing a point like so, "you are not going to slave away and catch the bus to work every day, while your boss flies on a private jet?" or "if you make all the money, why does your wife get to choose what house you will buy?". These are just a few examples. You will call upon your own creativity to find the phrase that suits your subject and goals.

NLP is really a study of "why." You can control the "why." You can question another person's "why." There is no way to fail at NLP, you can only gain knowledge and feedback. Each time you practice these skills, you will get a stronger sense of how to react and speak to different types of people. Since everyone is a little different, this is a great tool that can be used on anybody.

The best thing about learning NLP to influence or analyze your subject is that it allows you to view techniques that have been previously used on you, likely without your knowledge or consent. You will appreciate the skill to get what you want and to protect yourself against unwanted information or particularly effective sales pitches. Since NLP techniques are designed to test someone's subjective view on a topic, you can ask a simple question to change a negative view into a positive one. This can be done by saying, "how do you deal without having this (insert your desired result)?" When you are getting your answer, pay attention to how they breathe, and the gestures being used as they describe everything.

This could can the game in your personal relationships. You can have a harmonious relationship with you in the driver's seat. Your partner would never know because of your intimacy with them already.

Chapter 4

Deception

The average person tells several lies every day. We are trained to lie to protect ourselves. We lie to protect others. We lie to ourselves not even being aware of it. Just because it is extremely prevalent doesn't mean it isn't a great tool for manipulation. For example, how many white lies do parents tell their children to protect their innocence, or just to make them easier to deal with at the moment. Now, these white lies may be to protect them, but it is to control them for their own benefit. Most people can agree that lying to kids protects their innocence and is worth it, right?

The key is not to become a pathological liar, only lie when you have something to gain and a bulletproof story to back you up as well. You will want to nail down the details before ever repeating it to avoid mistakes. If you don't have time to plan out your lie effectively, telling the truth, even if it is a truth you don't approve of, is almost always going to be the better choice.

You can create an effective lie in several ways. You can leave details out of a story that is true, to mislead a person; emphasizing what you want them to hear. The key is that they believe you. You cannot mislead someone who does not believe what you are saying. Remember the truth is actually based on a person's perception of what matters to them and what they have already learned. Your job is to challenge that.

The truth is you are surrounded by deceitful people. You will look at their social media posts and see pictures of how much fun they are having and how happy their family looks, when actually, the pictures are orchestrated, and the family barely speaks to each other. Have you ever had a friend who was cheated on act like it is no big deal? Odds are they were actually devastated and may have even stopped believing in love. Now their life is just a show. Push play and go. Lies come in many forms. Your lies are forming a foundation for you to analyze a person on a deeper level, telling them whatever they want or need to hear. You should be observing and leading your subject.

During your job interview, didn't your potential employer talk about the company's values and goals, making it seem like you would be lucky to work there? In reality, they have no values, they don't give a crap about their employees, and you just found out that they lost half the staff in one year. Think back to the interview, how nervous you were wondering if you would be chosen. They were lying to you, and you did not care because of your personal goals at the time.

You might not even realize how much the people in your life have lied to you. You might at first think that this would be a horrible thing. However, the reason people lie varies and should not be taken personally. We think we know what is best for our loved ones, but sometimes they might surprise you, and the reasons might surprise you even more. This is why I encourage you to be deceitful to achieve what you want, because at the end of the day if you do not take control of your own life, someone else could be doing it for you. This is where your story is either a truth or a lie, a mix of both, depending on what you need someone to believe about you. Do not let others dictate your life by the stories they tell about you, especially to other people, you have to enforce your story by emphasizing what you want to be remembered for.

Starting your deception

Now it is your turn to enjoy lying; to master the universe with your narrative. You will create the world you want in your mind, and one lie at a time, make that world a reality.

The first important lie is that you care. You will have to work on your empathy. With all the other tools in this book, you should be on a good starting path to understanding how to read people. Empathy is a view taken on from your subject's perspective. You want to walk in their shoes. This gives you the window to know what it is that they really want to hear. You are trying to know what they know. Take an interest in your subject's hobbies or work. This display of interest is a path to telling them what you want them to think but in the context of what excites them. Try making a comparison to keep the momentum going.

Be sure that when setting your goal for your lie, you also set the stage. Start by examining your social media posts. Start posting things that interest your subject. They are likely to start to follow your posts. Update your profile. Get dressed up and ask a stranger to take a picture of you at the coffee shop. It will look like a friend took it and you are out having fun. Put on a flattering outfit, make sure it is still your style and check in somewhere trendy.

Find a cause that you can appear passionate about, but that is not too controversial. This will give you credit towards being viewed as a compassionate person. People will respect that you believe in something, and it will help you to appear to have depth as a person. Another way of making someone believe that you care about what they are saying is to ask a bunch of questions to analyze what their interests are. You can achieve this by asking about the types of books they like to read or what is their favorite city in the US. Have a few follow up questions ready.

Tell your own story

Write down what you want to be remembered for. Do you want to be known as a rich person, defined by money? Tell that story. Do you want to be remembered for being charitable? Tell that story. Do you want to be memorable in the first place?

It is important to be sure to tell your stories with care. I am going to tell you a story about my rich Aunt Betty. Aunt Betty made a lot of money suing people and writing stories for the gossip magazines of the 1990's. She put her money in the bank and a trust. She made me trustee, and I did not even know it. No one knew Aunt Betty had money. She drove a 15-year-old car. She never wore any jewelry. She drank cheap wine. She would complain about how expensive everything had become. She sold her house and moved into a small apartment after her seventieth birthday.

I thought my aunt was one of the happiest people I knew. She did not worry about too much, citing that it was out of her hands. She never had any of her own kids, but every year, she took her nieces and nephews to Disneyland. All the other family members thought she starved all year to afford that trip. We just went along with everything until one day she died. My mother told me she did not have anything valuable and a lawyer was taking care of her last bit of business she left behind. One night after work, I got a call from Aunt Betty's lawyer about her trust. I was in shock. Aunt Betty had a trust? This lawyer said he wasn't that far from my house and wanted me to sign the acceptance papers, which had a secrecy clause.

Aunt Betty had trusted me with her secret. She had a boatload of money, over a million dollars. To wrap this story up, she left it all to a charity. She paid me for making sure that the lawyer gave all the money to the charity. But I could never tell a soul how she deceived all of us. I admired her so much for being a con, I kept her secret. Besides, she paid me well.

At first, hearing about my Aunt Betty's trust, I felt bad for my mom and her siblings because they had no idea who their sister was. They thought she was a poor old woman who complained a lot. But instead, she was a generous person who believed that she should have money for a rainy day. She hated the thought of asking anyone for help. She wanted her leftover money to go to helping people. She believed her family could help themselves and that they would fight over money. She lied to them about her success, not outright, but in the form of a secret. In the end, a wonderful charity received money that would reach many needy people. That helped Aunt Betty sleep at night. Whatever your life goals are, you have to be willing to protect it, and deception might be the only way to keep others from sabotaging you.

People are so wrapped up in themselves that they will not even notice that you are not an open book, posting everything about yourself for the world to see. When you get questioned about your life, you will read the script that you wrote. You decide who you are, no one else. It is a good idea to have a few stories rehearsed. Rehearsing out loud is encouraged so that you can hear the tone and it will increase your chances of memorizing the stories. My personal favorite way to pull up a story to be able to relate to a person is to live vicariously through another person's story, making absolutely sure that the person you are telling the story to does not know the person who you stole the story from.

The point is that sometimes the truth does not serve you or your goals. Once you feel comfortable with this idea, things will get a lot easier for you. People do not need to know everything about us, just to be able to use it against us at a later time. You will be smarter than that. Let your target fall for that and reveal themselves for you to influence. That is why I say; the world is yours because you can literally transform it. Get to work on writing your "script."

Tips for lying effectively

Crank up the empathy: Before you start bending the truth for your own benefit, it is crucial that you have already formed an emotional bond with the other party as this will make them far more likely to believe you. This means you need to come on strong, right from the beginning as it typically only takes about two minutes for a person to decide if they like someone they have just met. If you fall on the wrong side of this initial appraisal then you are going to have a much more difficult time of convincing them of anything, even the truth.

As such, you are going to want to watch any new target you are considering beforehand to get the clearest picture of their personality type as possible. Once you have a general idea of how they think and act, you can then introduce a version of yourself that matches their expectations, making anything else you need to do far more manageable as a result.

Know common tells: The reason that most people get caught when they lie is that they telegraph their actions without even realizing it. As such, if you hope to ever deceive others effectively, then you are going to want to learn then, so you can learn to avoid using them. The most common tells that show someone is lying include odd hand gestures, looking away from the person target of the conversation, speaking too quickly and pausing before speaking. If you can remove these from your own behaviors while telling a lie, then there will be less of a gap between the question and the answer and less of a reason for the person you are speaking with not to trust you.

Watch your body language: When a person tells a lie, they commonly adopt a defensive, closed posture. As such, a great way to assure the other party that you are not lying is to adopt open body language instead. This includes things like standing with your arms causally at your sides which says you are open to the conversation that you are a part of and are anxious to come to a consensus. You will also want to ensure that you stand facing them and slowly move closer to them as you continue the conversation. Finally, you will want to ensure you don't place anything that could be considered a barrier between you, even if it is just a file folder.

Your hands are also very important, especially when you are interacting with someone new. Studies show that gesturing with your hands makes other people more likely to believe whatever it is you are saying. Likewise, a firm, non-aggressive handshake is important to starting off anything more than a causal relationship on the right foot.

Conclusion

Thank you for making it through to the end of *How to Analyze People: Dark Psychology - Secret Techniques to Analyze and Influence Anyone Using Body Language, Human Psychology, and Personality Types*, let's hope it was informative and able to provide you with all of the tools you need to achieve your goals, whatever it is that they may be. Just because you've finished this book doesn't mean there is nothing left to learn on the topic, expanding your horizons is the only way to find the mastery you seek.

The next step, however, is to stop reading already and to get ready to follow through on using the techniques discussed in the previous chapters to your benefit and also to not just understand but to really believe that you are the only one who can change your experiences in this lifetime. You do not have to worry about if people will like you or not because now you can control that. Enjoy this new freedom. Preserve your skills for years of use. I hope that I was able to make a difference in your chances of getting what you want. You should have no trouble with the right amount of discipline and practice. The results of your use of these techniques will depend on the amount effort you put into applying them. Remember, knowledge is power put actions are fruitful.

There will be many people in your life that you will not want to use this on. However, you might want to share the book with others if you see them struggling. This book was written for any audience because we are all manipulated every day, and it is a crystal ball to the questions of "how?" and "why?" Not many people are aware of that this even happens to them.

I hope you use this information responsibly. It is powerful and has been in used for centuries. If you pass this information on, do it thoughtfully. You have the whole world in front of you, and it is yours to play with. No one should be able to pull the wool over your head now that you are in tune with how this works. You will definitely recognize when it is happening to you.

Thank you

Before you go, I just wanted to say thank you for purchasing my book.

You could have picked from dozens of other books on the same topic but you took a chance and chose this one.

So, a HUGE thanks to you for getting this book and for reading all the way to the end.

Now I wanted to ask you for a small favor. **Could you please take just a few minutes to leave a review for this book on Amazon?**

This feedback will help me continue to write the type of books that will help you get the results you want. So if you enjoyed it, please let me know.

CPSIA information can be obtained
at www.ICGtesting.com
Printed in the USA
FSHW011458260120
66497FS